THE BOOK
THAT NO ONE
SHOULD READ!

THE BOOK THAT NO ONE SHOULD READ!

ALAN SHINKFIELD

Copyright © Alan Shinkfield.

All rights reserved. No part of this book may be reproduced in any form or by any electronic or mechanical means, including information storage and retrieval systems, without permission in writing from the publisher, except by reviewers, who may quote brief passages in a review.

ISBN: 978-1-63732-524-7   (Paperback Edition)
ISBN: 978-1-63732-525-4   (Hardcover Edition)
ISBN: 978-1-63732-523-0   (E-book Edition)

Scripture quotations marked NIV are taken from the Holy Bible, New International Version®. NIV®. Copyright © 1973, 1978, 1984 by International Bible Society. Used by permission of Zondervan. All rights reserved. [Biblica]

Book Ordering Information

Phone Number: 315 288-7939 ext. 1000 or 347-901-4920
Email: info@globalsummithouse.com
Global Summit House
www.globalsummithouse.com

Printed in the United States of America

The Chapters

1 – It Existed Before It Became Visible! 1
2 – The Time Before History! 12
3 – Evolution: A Common Sense Approach! 22
4 – Some Truths For The Young! 30
5 – The Black Angel! 38
6 – The Large Millstone 48

Introducing All Those People Who Should Not Read This Book And The Reasons Why They Shouldn't!

ME, THE AUTHOR, because the comments included, show that I am a judgemental person and not pure in myself.

MEN, because they will have to admit they are not here to dominate women, but rather to love and protect them.

WOMEN, because they must recognise that both sexes were created equal, and that they are equal not superior to men.

CHRISTIANS, because they are sinners and not perfect, they have lost the plot and do not dedicate their lives to the service of their God, not just Sunday (Sabbath) Worship.

ATHEISTS, Because there may be something written in this book that will change their way of thinking and accept that there is a God.

AGNOSTICS, because even if it is in their own ego, they must believe in something.

SPORTSPEOPLE, because at sometime in their lives they will realise that being a celebrity does have an impact on the young, and that their sporting lives and high earning capacity must eventually end.

THE GAY COMMUNITY, because they can never be anything but church goers unless they embrace true and honest, and lasting repentance.

THE ELDERLY, because in a hopeless world they could find true hope in a Christ filled new world.

SPORTING SUPPORTERS, because of their one eyed evaluation, they may miss the incredible talent and ability of players in the opposing team. Their allegiance to their team can border an deep hatred for other players who have the complete support of their own team supporters.

REFEREES AND UMPIRES, because in all honesty this book does stand behind men who are only human and can make mistakes. This fact may have a serious effect on the rhythm of their hearts, which is not intended.

THE HANDICAPPED, because of all people, they accept their disability with dignity. They need little encouragement from this writer, for they have their own body of enthusiastic supporters.

THE RICH, because they may discover that money and material things may not buy you a passport to eternal life, but that you may have to live the meagre existence, in the afterlife, that your fellow humans have suffered, in earthly life, without help from you.

THE POOR, because you have already lived in hell on earth, believe in God and live a Holy and sheltered life in Heaven.

THE SCIENTIFIC COMMUNITY, because you believe that your knowledge exceeds the bounds of earthly learning, so therefore you are gods.

DRUG USERS, because you accept your power to abstain whenever and wherever and what ever you are addicted too, you may never accept that you are addicted, no matter what proof is placed before you.

TEACHERS & PREACHERS, because you have gained learning from others who have gone before and therefore you are very seldom equipped with life's real experiences. You become changeless.

P PLATERS, because they believe that they are invincible, they cannot accept that other road users do cause accidents. They then must become aware of other motorist disregard for road rules and drive accordingly.

USERS OF OH MY GOD OR OMG., because they call on a Deity that they do not accept or believe in, unknowingly they are committing blasphemy and disregarding the power of the very One they are calling upon.

ALL PEOPLE, because you are living in an age that cares for the present, and are unaware or uncaring of what the future holds.

STRONG CHURCHES, because of their inward vision and not an outreach to the wider community, they miss the mission for which they exist. For example, in a city where thousands attend weekly services, that city still sponsors a Gay and Lesbian Parade.

TRUTH SEEKERS, because in most cases they can't handle the truth, and do not admit to a corrupt society.

SMALL CHURCHES, because they delight in an increase in congregation members, but deny their obligation to work outside their worship centre where most sinners needing God's forgiveness are.

THE SHEPHERDS, because they are too busy feeding themselves with rich spiritual food, and their charges are left wandering around seeking wholesome nourishment and receiving trampled food and muddied water.

ALL YOUTH, because I have made the same mistakes as you are now, I spent money on material things and wasted money. When I got married and had children of my own, I needed that which I had wasted.

AND ABOVE ALL YOU! Because you may be awakened to monumental untruths regarding the creation of the world and all that is in it. The greatest danger that could happen is that you will rely on your own common sense.

It Existed Before It Became Visible!

It does not matter where we look, it does not matter what we use in our every day life, it existed before it became visible. Every invention that has aided and added to our comfort, benefit, or enjoyment existed before it materialised.

It existed in someone's mind, then onto a drawing board and then to an engineer, a manufacturer until it was last seen as the finished product. The car you drive, the road you drive on, the bridge that gives you safe passage over rivers and waterways, all existed before they became visible and serviceable.

The committee you serve on, the club you support came to being after it existed in someone's mind, but as every idea, unless it shows progress through many processes it will wither and die. The program becomes real, alive and then visible when it is approved by people willing to plan, work and sacrifice time and effort for the project.

The same is with all things including creation, there was God, His Son, heaven, there were angels, all in existence before the earth, and all its wonders the sky, stars, moon and sun, became visible.

Man's mind is too feeble to grasp the full truth of how the earth was created, so man fabricated stories that placed these far above the comprehension of ordinary people.

Unfortunately the human mind has accepted these theories and the Christian Church has done nothing to face the truth and argue against these fallacies. So the Evolution theory, and that is all it is, a theory, a figment of man's fertile imagination, is now taught throughout the world's entire school system. To a simple mind and common sense there is little or no proof that it happened by the evolution story.

There are so many things that exist in today's world because someone had a bright idea, or in some cases just wanted to obtain fame of fortune. It then becomes important that we test and examine every proposal that requires an input of our funds for investment, before we accept it as being true and achievable.

There are concepts that may have existed in a person's mind, but because of laziness or impatience, they never took the necessary steps to see it to fruition and it became viable and visible. We are susceptible to accepting what seems to be an excellent opportunity without considering if it is workable, attainable, has it been tried before and, if so was it successful?

All these important facts must be considered before we entrust our good name, our hard earned finances, and perhaps in extreme circumstances our total future, to projects that may never reach completion. I have always believed that confidence tricksters have brilliant concepts sometimes, unfortunately they do not possess the know-how or patience to see it materialise.

In desperation they sell the idea only to unsuspecting investors. Many of these proposals are accepted because they seem to have prospects for success, in the hands of a honest and knowledgeable person would net them and their investors a handsome profit.

So it is with the teachings of God in the Bible, it is important to accept that the original history book is the Bible. The intermingled history of Egypt, Rome and the countries both ancient and present day, around the Mediterranean Sea are all linked. The great flood recorded in Genesis chapters 6 to 9, is proven by the footprints of now extinct animals.

Fame is not always bestowed on completely honest people, there are many religious sects based entirely on one persons proclamation. We are now saddled with the assumption of prehistoric animals. How dare we assume and accept this as fact, when there is no recorded history to substantiate that as fact.

Christianity offers and promises so much and yet without any consideration at all, is cast aside. The evolution assumption is accepted without calls for a time span of where and when and time the world evolved to what we know today. It must also be considered that the ancients were able to build structures without the aid of modern machinery.

There is speculation of periods of five hundred million years down to one million years, would it take so long for the development to what we have today, when we consider the enormous strides taken in the last one hundred years? We should ask evolutionists to show the procedure of change, they have shown us the transition from ape to man, but not how ape became a resident of earth. They tell us that two plankton merged and we in human form eventuated. They omitted to detail the intricacies that form the human body.

They search under the ground for traces of past life, and tell about prehistoric times, but how could there be pre historic times. This in itself means times before recorded history. The Bible not only tells how but why, and is backed up by other nations history. Its listings of the generations of the Hebrew people can, when added together give us a believable time frame the world as we know it existed. But don't forget it existed in God's planning before it became visible.

It is well to relive the earliest times of recorded Biblical history, to walk with real, not imaginary people. To find how events recorded in the Old Testament can be proven by simple facts found today. New Testament history can take us back over two thousand years and allow us to walk in with Jesus and his disciples. Much wisdom and modern day sayings can be traced back to Israel's King David and King Solomon, and if you have not read these portions of Scripture, then you are poor in the written and spoken words. There is a beauty which over the years has been replaced by the common bad language of this day and age.

Here another point should be considered, as we have seen that every thing exists, in someone's thoughts before it becomes visible, so does temptation, it is not a sin until it is materialised. One old hymn presented the words, **"Yield not to temptation, for yielding is sin,"** the thoughts we have but never carry out, adds up to a victory for Christ. Did I exist before I became visible, My life in the womb was hidden, but that is not what I am referring too. Was I a part of God's plan?

Was I destined to become the youngest of three children to my mother and father? Was this a tapestry of my life woven in heaven? Was I chosen to live the life I have and was it predestined? Were men and women like Whitefield, Spurgeon the Wesley brothers, and in the modern age Bishop Tutu, Billy Graham, Martin Luther

King and the dedication to the less fortunate in India, Mother Teresa ordained by God before the Womb.

Does this sound so absurd to the trained minds of today, but both John the Baptist and Jesus were promised well before they became visible to those around them, so why shouldn't some people be ordained before birth to do God's work while living a normal life of service? The reason for your birth may be hidden even from you, but there was a reason, but also you were granted a free will, to travel, you may love, you may hate, or you can live the predestined life planned for you even before you became visible.

Predestined, is one word that many Christians cannot accept and agree upon, but it simply means that your birth to this world has a pre-existing plan, because of your given free will you are not forced to follow that plan and most people do not. Here lies a huge problem with the Christian Church, we are so involved in arguing about concepts between ourselves and forget who our real enemy is, Satan! How he must rejoice when he sees his enemy divided and the huge forces for good are not united but divided.

Remember Jesus warned us about this. Some scholars are convinced the John did not write the Book of Revelation, is this earth shattering. does it really matter? Although you may chose to follow your own direction, you will be judged on the guidance of God. There is no doubt that God uses people to glorify His name and extend His Kingdom on earth.

These people are chosen, trained, granted sufficient wisdom to perform the task allotted to them. Learning may come from education, text books, prescribed courses and the teaching profession, however wisdom is a gift from God and is gathered over a time of life's experiences through which you have been.

Were these extraordinary people or were they designed by a higher power to become visible and change lives? The Lay-person, never identified, who challenged a young Charles Spurgeon, those Germans who demonstrated enormous faith by singing hymns when a terrible storm hit their ship and so gave an example to John Wesley. Perhaps the New York Missionary who commenced a lunch time prayer meeting with six people and saw it grow until there were 50,000 attending like prayer meetings in New York City. There was the young man who saw me sitting in a gutter, bemoaning about a flat tyre on the car, he told me to go home get dressed and go to church with him.

I did and that lead to my conversion over sixty years ago. The universe exists and according scientists is still growing, my reservations about the huge amounts of money spent on space exploration, but now realise without this, the great wonders of the universe would be lost to mankind. How dare any one put forward the suggestion that two non existing elements caused a big bang. This universe in beyond human comprehension.

I also accept that I will lose my earthly existence, but what has been and is still being prepared for all true believers in the only Living God, the promised paradise, will take us an eternity to identify with its huge unimaginable wonder. The immense size of the universe compared to the smallness of mankind gives one the humbleness which enables them to worship a God who created it all, and with all sincerity place their lives and future in such amazing and awesome hands.

There are many facts concerning ancient kingdoms that are verified in the Bible. Name changes have happened and are still happening today. Kingdoms that existed are named in the Old Testament. Egypt's history are intertwined with the history of Israel. As is the Babylonian, Assyrian, Hittite, Mendes, Persian again proves the existence of the Hebrew state and shows the Bible reflects the true history of the area.

Places we recognise now were listed in the Bible, Rome, Syria, Egypt, Crete, Greece, Iran, Cyprus are just a few. Perhaps the oldest of these would be the Egyptian dated from 2600 until 650 BC. Whilst we are on that, as though there are moves to rid the calendar of BC., and AD., we still date our calendar on the birth of Christ. If we can accept this fact then why can't we accept that Jesus did live in this world?

We can date the years of the Hebrew nation because of the Bible's record of the ages of the generations in the book of Genesis, from where do the evolutionists calculate their millions of years?

If we deny our young people the opportunity to at least give them the knowledge of an alternate plan other than evolution, their education is simply put not complete. We take for granted the modern marvels of our scientific discoveries, These are so named because they were always there but not yet visible or usable. Humanity cannot claim to invented electricity because electrical storms were always part of the earthly environment.

We did however produce, harness and use it for the benefit of all mankind. When through cyclones, storms and fierce winds we loose power, remember that this is just an introduction into how reliant we are on flicking a switch. Can you say we invented the atom? No! We discovered it and turned it into a killing agent far above anything man has developed before. Again we harnessed it to produce electricity, but we were not aware of its potential to damage and even destroy human lives. We did not invent coal we (man) discovered that it had many uses and utilised it for heating, providing energy and it is now probably the world's most used energy source. Also these base products were present before they were recognised, existed and used as power bases for entertainment, comfort and jobs which in turn provide the standard of living we can attain today.

The minerals used in modern day appliances and work related machinery, were not an invention of man but a discovery. They have existed since the beginning of the world, all man did after the discovery was to utilise them to his needs. When we look back and find that history had ways of constructing and manufacturing basic machinery, modern man used these primitive ideas to build those we have today. If we look at the evolution of the computer and acknowledge the updating and improvements, the size, from specially constructed rooms, and almost exclusively for governments and big business, reduced to fit in your pocket and available to all.

The materials used existed before the first computer hit the design board. When considered all discoveries and the following use of these in design inventions have made man to consider that he is able to control the world. But the danger from this mode of thinking that all things do not come from his knowledge, but from his ego and his vanity to believe in his own self sufficiency.

The earliest forms of mechanical transport relied on wood, fire and water, all in existence before man was able to harness them to his advantage, these things are listed in the Bible. Without all these base forms of energy man could not have designed and manufactured the products in use today.

Whereas it is a modern miracle that we have these machines as servants, the drawback is financial. To obtain such appliances both husband and wife must continue to work to meet their financial commitments. The days of being a full time parent has gone, children when they need the care and love of both parents have to be content with child care facilities.

My mother heated her washing water in a copper with wood fire, she cooked on a stove powered by fire and wood, we warmed the house by wood and heated our bathwater in a chip (wood) heater. The cost of purchasing or cutting our own wood was reasonable and the exercise beneficial.

In this age of overweight and obesity, lack of fitness through over refined processed food, but then lack of exercise plays a major part. In honesty, compare flicking an electric switch or lighting a gas burner to cutting a pile of wood, and judge for yourself which expends the more energy? Does every modern convenience make us to dependant on them and not our given physical and mental powers?

Turn off your computer and think for yourself, leave your calculator and grab a pencil and paper to work out your finances, for one week use your own devises and remember what you did when the power went off in the last storm. What did you do? Could you last for a week?

In summary, every thing that existed before it became visible and therefore useful, has not always been to enhance mankind's life on earth. There are life saving and worthwhile advances in medicine. The transport in public movers, motor vehicles move many quicker in better comfort, but can become lethal weapons in the wrong hands.

Splitting the atom has caused death and destruction to many thousands of communities like ours and even in peace time can devastate not only the present generation but generations to come. When we discover a new product there must be wiser heads honestly seeking, is it worth the trouble, hardship, death and destruction it could cause.

What is needed is true Christian thinking for today to make sure that what we discover and use has no ill effects on our fellow humans. Asbestos, regarded as a boon to many industries was identified as a killer in America back in 1932.

I worked in the building materials industry in the early 1980's where asbestos was still used. We must not let power and greed for financial gain overpower these precious gifts that existed before the became visible to man and the true potential was identified. Unless we look to placing Biblical truths into modern day practice, we will never be able to accept that Christianity is as relevant and indeed necessary as it was when its King and Master walked the earth.

We teach our children about pre-historic monsters, and don't teach them about practical economics, as proven by huge mobile phone accounts. The facts that world markets are as stable as the governments that lead them. Your children are being inducted into a society which denies the opportunity of comparing and proving as I did, that God lives. They are being lead away from truth to following a hypothesis which places its foundation far beyond the comprehension of ordinary people.

Another tale similar to the Emperor's new clothes. If you don't accept it you are a fool. Our children deserve the right to know that the world financial markets are effected by recessions and depressions and do happen from time to time. They must be made aware that if every one went to draw their money from established banks, because of the banks investments, they may not be able to fulfil their commitment to protect your money.

We cannot and should not, lull our young people into a position of believing it cannot happen in our country in this day and age. It can and will whilst money rules the world wide markets. Our Christian Church has a huge part to play as helpmates assisting with family financial problems, teaching the young how to manage financial windfalls, or where sickness and death are placing extreme financial hardship on the remaining partner and children. The first lesson should be don't spend what you haven't got.

Yet we still take the recognition and glory for things that could never have eventuated if it was not for a Creator God who placed everything in place for our benefit. The theory of two elements and a big bang, my feeble mind asks, where and how did these two elements appear if before there was nothing? Therefore for want of a more factual thesis, I accept there is a Creator God, and when the magnitude of the whole universe is considered, a big bang did eventuate. There had to be something in existence before it became visible. How God came into being is far beyond my comprehension, but I know He did and still does exist.

If we don't teach Bible stories and the truth of Christianity then we are not completing the education people deserve and will at sometime need. There are different directions in life we can take if we don't know them how do we know what we want to do or be.

The Time Before History!

I do not believe in pre-history, because I am not persuaded that nothing happened that wasn't recorded. Creation, no mater if you follow the evolution theory or the true creation by God, was the beginning of everything, including history. The Bible records the formation of the world - sun - moon - stars - animals - birds - fish and reptiles even to man and woman.

Without seeking to cause disagreement between man and woman, the Bible tells that woman was made from man, with a rib taken as the base, this does not make man in any way superior to woman. What it should prove is their comparability as their origin was from the one source.

The human mind was not made to comprehend nothing, yet both schools of thought require us to understand nothingness. Evolutionists would have you believe that two elements came together, created a big bang, but do not explain how the two elements evolved from nothing. Creationists believe in a mighty Spirit who created all the wonders of the world in six days.

Some scholars have termed the pre-historic period as covering, creation, Adam and Eve, Cain and Abel, Noah and the Ark, and the Tower of Babel. All of these are not pre-history because they are recorded in Genesis the first book of the Bible. We cannot dispute the fact that somehow and in someway the world and the universe were created from nothing.

There has to be a first, nothing can exist without a first of the species, there has to be a male and female to generate life. The fact that I exist is proof positive that a man and woman came together. Scientists and some of the medical profession have made claims to cloning and assisting those that were barren and could not produce offspring, to give birth to and raise children.

This they could not do unless they obtained the egg and sperm required and begot descendants. There are many facts that lead me to believe that the Bible stories are true. Noah and the flood a reliable instance. Scientists, evolutionists, archaeologists and others did dig through clay and find, what they claim are prehistoric bones, which they age in millions of years.

In their diggings, in many places throughout the world, they refuse to recognise that what they are digging through is the positive proof that there was a world wide flood in which Noah his family and selected animals were safely transported above the waters. All other living creatures were drowned and covered with a thick residue of mud. This is the same as today as mud from floods covers everything that cannot or does not move.

It is important to recognise the Bible truths as the history of the Jewish people, and that this history is closely lined to world history. These are the ancestors of the Israelites; About 1900 B. C. Abraham came to Canaan, his son Isaac is born. Isaac has a son named Jacob, this is important for Jacob has twelve sons and these are the ancestors of he twelve tribes of Israel.

The history of two nations now become entwined as Joseph the most prominent of Jacob's sons is appointed as an advisor to the Egyptian King. These twelve tribes are mentioned in the Book of Revelation chapter 7 and verses 5 to 8. ***"From the tribe of Judah 12,000 were sealed, from the tribe of Reuben 12,000, from the tribe of Gad 12,000, from the tribe of Asher 12,000, from the tribe of Naphtali 12,000, from the tribe of Manasseh 12,000, from the tribe of Simeon 12,000, from the tribe of Levi 12,000, from the tribe of Issachar 12,000, from the tribe of Zebulun 12,000, from the tribe of Joseph 12,000, from the tribe of Benjamin 12,000.***

These are the same family members written about in Genesis chapter 37, so historically they were mentioned in the first and last Books of the Bible. Through recorded history we know that the Israelites were enslaved in Egypt, both Biblical and Egyptian history records these facts. The Bible records how God raised a leader, Moses, chosen to lead the descendants of Jacob out of Egypt's slavery. Through the history recorded in the Bible we know that the Israelites wandered through the wilderness for some forty years from 1250 B.C., and to 1210 B.C.

We also know that God did not allow Moses to set foot in the Promised Land, and that Joshua lead the first stage of the invasion of Canaan, and that these people were ruled by people appointed as Judges. The Old Testament book of Judges covers the events that transpired under these Judges, perhaps the most famous being Samson. This was a lawless period in Jewish history before the monarchy was established.

The reign of King Saul saw a united Israelite kingdom established, King Saul reigned from B.C. 1030 until 1010. King David followed Saul, and we remember David as the one that killed the giant Philistine with a sling shot, and he reined from 1010 until 970.

His son Solomon reined from 970 till 931, after Solomon, two Israelite kingdoms were established, in the north, Israel under King Rehoboam and in the south, Judah reined by King Jeroboam.

What now I am proving that we accept the history as written, about the Persian Empire, and therefore should accept that the Jews were taken and exiled in Babylonia. In 538 B.C. Cyrus allowed the Jews to return to Jerusalem, the new Temple was commenced and the walls restored in 445 - 443 B.C. History also tells that in 333 B.C. Alexander the Great established Greek rule in the eastern region of the Mediterranean.

The Ptolemies, descendants of Alexander's generals ruled this region from 323 to 198 B.C. And then the area was ruled by Seleucids also descendants of Alexander's generals. The revolution in Israel was headed by Judas Maccabeus and re-established Jewish independence, the Judas family and descendants called the Hasmoneans ruled from 166 till 63 B.C. It was in 63 B.C., a Roman general, Pompey conquered Israel and it is now ruled by kings appointed from Rome.

The first of these was Herod the Great and he ruled from 37 to 4 B.C. All these are historical facts and should be accepted as world history and proof that the Bible records so much of this history it cannot be wrong. The creation story in Genesis 2: 4 to 6.

"When the Lord God made the earth and the heavens - and no shrub of the field had yet appeared on the earth and no plant of the field had yet sprung up. For the Lord God had not sent rain on the earth and there was no man to work the ground, but streams came up from the earth and watered the whole surface of the ground." Does this prove that the writer knew what we now know that there is a reservoir of underground water?

This account of creation is somewhat more detailed than in Genesis chapter 1, it is as it the writer wanted to give a description that showed there was nothing, no trees, shrubs or plants because of a lack of water and there was no one to work the land. We can clearly see that there were two authors of the creation story, who wrote them?

It could not have been a man, for we are told that there was no man to work the ground. The answer is in the first chapter of this book, it existed in God's heaven before it became visible on earth, the writer, then was one of the heavenly bodies who witnessed it all. Recorded history is accepted without question, but history printed in the Bible is not, and yet we can find absolute proof that stories in the Bible are true by joining the histories of other empires together.

In the histories of other empires and countries there are some acts that, they would prefer not to be made public. By comparing the Roman advance into Israel we find that in B.C. 63 the Roman Empire expanded and the Jewish race once more were over powered and ruled by outsiders.

We also have already noted that Herod the Great ruled as king up to 4 B. C. Roman history would show that Jesus was brought before the Roman governor who was Pilate, we know that the Romans preferred their captured nations to be content and not be troublesome. For this they went out of their way to appease the leaders of the Synagogue, who were accepted by the masses as their spiritual leaders.

To gather further facts together we know that the Romans were cruel, and their form of capital punishment was crucifixion, history and Hollywood have shown us the savagery of the entertainment provided in the various Roman arenas.

We can trace through the Roman and Bible history that there was a man named Jesus, who preached throughout Jerusalem and beyond. We know that the leaders of the Synagogue paid Judas to betray

Jesus, and that his so-called trial ended in the crucifixion. We also know that the leaders of the established church were those who devised the betrayal, capture, trial and eventual crucifixion of Jesus the son of God, because he was a threat to their power over the masses.

These Rabbis and priests had ample proof of the great power that Jesus had over the people of the day who followed him, and glorified him on his triumphant ride into Jerusalem, and realised the great threat that these very people posed to their power and high positions. So Judas, who it is believed was the treasurer and was approached with the bribe of thirty pieces of silver to betray Jesus.

Why was it necessary to have someone to betray Jesus? Hadn't he walked through the streets of the cities, and preached in the country? He was easily recognised as proven by the Samaritan women at the well, so why did it take a kiss to identify Jesus, the one who Judas had followed? Like so many stories in the Bible, they are paralleled by every day occurrences, how better to bring down an opponent than to have them betrayed by one of his own.

The betrayal of Jesus by Judas could have launched the on the spot decision made by the crowd in seeking the release of Barabbas instead of the King and Messiah for whom they had waited. We may think that we have exclusive license to selfish acts when we consider the moral state of the world today, but in reading the Bible you will see that selfishness and jealousy has been with even the most dedicated. David's lust for Bathsheba, the leaders of the Synagogue, in wanting Jesus dead, King Saul's feelings toward David, Jacob's other sons' hatred of Joseph, even the disciples feelings toward the Samaritans.

We are truly descendants of all those who have gone before, some are servants of the Heavenly Father, whilst others are slaves to the dark and evil one. History has shown us that Solomon had great wisdom, he invented the phrase, "what goes around comes around, there is nothing new under the sun. Sure some things have changed, we kill with guns instead of swords, whereas war was the greatest killer of people, we now have motor vehicles in the hands of unthinking selfish people.

They can now kill, injure, maim, we can now loose our good nature and name by the indulgence in drugs and liquor, without any immediate feelings for another's rights, we are prepared to take away their future.

How can you accept that the Romans invaded England and built cities and waterways, communal baths and not accept that armies of the same country conquered Israel? How can so called learned people not accept the historical time frame and not accept that the same regime could crucify a honest and innocent man? No man has the right to study and then alter to their own satisfaction what they have learned!

How can we accept today that the justice system is not always correct in its deliberation, that the lust for power drives dictatorships to enforce harsh and unjust punishment on its peoples, and yet deny that the same lust for power caused lies to be fabricated, and the crucifixion of the worlds only perfect inhabitant, Jesus Christ?

Why do we accept way-out theories and unauthenticated statements and yet deny the existence of a God, who by experiences in practising Christians' lives, does exist, does care and wants nothing but a perfect world? Only you have the right to chose the way you travel, but never loose sight of the fact there is always an alternate route to arrive at your destination.

Only you have the freedom and God given right to follow the goodness and love of God or the hate and ultimate destruction of our souls through Satan the evil one.

All should be aware that Satan was an angel and had all the privileges of a servant of God. It is believed that he was the chief musician who was not content with being subservient to Almighty God that he lead a revolution, and with his followers lost the battle and was cast out of heaven to earth and which he has tried to rule his way ever since.

As Satan and his followers lost the battle in heaven and he lost the battle on earth with the resurrection of Jesus Christ. Jesus overcame death and his resurrection paved the way for the Biblical prophesy, that he would come again to judge all that have ever inhabited our world. So now death has lost its sting for true believers have gained eternal life through the promises of God's only Son Jesus Christ.

From this we can believe that all these things the lust for greed, power and condoning of selfishness, all are a part of history and if you prefer prehistory, for what Satan started in heaven he continues on earth. His principles of putting his lust for absolute power, saw him and his followers defeated in heaven and will see him and his earthly followers defeated on earth with the return of Jesus Christ. Who is a follower of Satan on earth?

Anyone who does not accept Jesus Christ as their Saviour and the only Son of God. If only our minds were flexible enough at study and accept the truth of God's promises in Malachi 3 verses 8 to 10; *"Will a man rob God? Yet you rob me. But you ask, 'How do we rob you?' In tithes and offerings. You are under a curse - the whole nation of you - because you are robbing me.*

Bring the whole tithe into the storehouse, that there may be food in my house. 'Test me in this' says the Lord God almighty, 'and see if I will not throw open the floodgates of heaven and pour out so much blessing that you will not have room for it.'"

Leviticus 26 verses 3 to 6; *"If you follow my decrees and are careful to obey my commands, I will send you rain in its season, and the ground will yield its crops and the trees of the field their fruit. Your threshing will continue until grape harvest and the grape harvest will continue until planting, and you will eat all the food you want and live in safety in by our land."*

In about 520 BC., the Lord God spoke through the prophet Haggai, Chapter 1 and verses 5 to 7, and this is as true now as then, so take warning, *"Now this is what the Lord Almighty says: Give careful thoughts to your ways. You have planted much, but have harvested little. You eat, but never have enough. You drink, but never have your fill. You put on clothes, but are not warm. You earn wages, only to put them in a purse with holes in it.*

I am not a prophet and yet I can see money and finance being the tool to bringing about the world's downfall. Now we can blame the banks but these are buildings, the management is left your fellow man, who forget how difficult it is to enjoy life on a fixed wage. Once it was individuals who earned a place in the debtors prison, now it is nations, countries and businesses. We deny our children nothing and have credit cards to ensure that their wants are satisfied.

Insurance companies also are blamed for lack of compassion, but again it is faceless men and women who decide the fate of their fellow workers. Why is the details in insurance company's conditions in small writing? Because we know the company, but not those top brass who will have the final decision.

I again turn to Haggai, to show that what comes around goes around, 2 verses 6 to 9. *"This is what the Lord Almighty says: 'In a little while I will once more shake the heavens and the earth, the sea and the dry land. I will shake all nations, and the desired of all nations will come, and I will fill this house with glory,' says the Lord Almighty. The silver is mine and the gold is mine," declares their Lord Almighty.*

Consider recent events in New Zealand, Japan, floods, earthquakes, volcanoes erupting, this is God's warning us to repent as did all the population of Nineveh in the book of Jonah, as recorded in Chapter one. The present day church has forgotten two words which are necessary to fight against the evil that surrounds us, repentance and revival. Revival is as dependent on repentance as repentance is to revival.

Two other words in the Christian vocabulary that are completely reliant upon each other, are faith and prayer. You cannot successfully pray without complete faith in a living God whose Son died on a cross that our sins would be forgiven. Your faith cannot exist without prayer, other words that are inseparable, sin and forgiveness. Sin is the breaking of God's ordnances, which we all have done, forgiveness was won by the sacrifice of Jesus Christ on the cross of Calvary.

Evolution: A Common Sense Approach!

It wasn't till after a motor vehicle accident which left me a chronic pain sufferer, and I was referred to a psychiatrist that I learned I had an IQ of 122. It was then I heard about Solomon and prayed for wisdom, It was some years ago and now these are the answers I receive.

We have all seen the drawings of man's evolution from ape to what we are today, the question I pose is this, if man evolved from ape why are there still apes today? If the evolutionist's answer is that there are now two different species, then why is there no record of pre-historic man being seen today as depicted in the drawings?

Why are we interested in disproving a God when we accept things that are but a figment of man's fertile imagination, and there is no positive proof whatsoever of such a radical change? How excited do we get when there is another find of ancient bones embedded in dry mud?

I fail to grasp these are all so called relics of a bygone age, these is no doubt that they lived. Does it ever come to mind to ask why bones of animals known to us today are not also found? Would it dent the evolution theory to find bones of these animals with out any sign that they also were victims of what ever covered the earth in mud? Perhaps it is because I have listened to many theories on how to do things, many of them false, that I fail to accept any, without careful study and perusal.

Why hasn't the prospect of massive animals being extinct because the earth could not sustain them? Even today, as man encroaches on the habitats of elephants, that their food chain dwindles. I would turn your attention to the ruins of Pompeii after the eruption of the volcano, those not able to escape were embalmed for ever in a layer of lave.

We have all seen the pictures of these unfortunates in magazines, books and on television. Then why is it not accepted by scholars that Noah's flood trapped all these beasts whose bones we dig up from under the mud? We have for too long allowed the evolutionist to alter facts to suit their own theories. They have no written or past-on verbal proof of any of their deductions.

These are simple elementary truths which are changed and expounded by a few but believed by many, and why? Because it is easier to accept what someone has told us than peruse the facts ourselves.

If you ask even the youngest angler what happens when fish die, you will find the answer, they float. To verify this fact you only have to watch television news to see dead fish floating on top of the water, and this would mean their remains would not be embedded in mud unless they were smothered by a mud slide caused by a gigantic flood.

Life styles have changed, in my youth I spent holidays with my cousins on their parent's farm, and noticed differences in the farm animals. The cows were plump and had heavy heads short legs and ate grass. Horses mainly were sleek, speedy and attractive to the eye, their usefulness was directed to transport, by riding or pulling a cart. Their heads were upright giving them good vision at speed. Pigs I noticed were usually rotund, had short legs because they loved getting down into it.

Dogs on the farm were built for speed and were able to round up a herd of sheep and drive them to where the farmer wanted them. Sheep on the other hand were made to be guided to the required place.

Not wishing to learn the tasks my cousins had participated in since the time they could walk, I was considered as just another useless city boy. So I had much spare time to ponder why these animals had been fitted with the requirements needed to carry out and fulfil their destiny.

Had the cow had a long neck as the horse, it would gain a sore neck bending it to reach the grass unless its front legs were shorter than its back legs. If the horse had a short neck as the cow has, its visibility would have been reduced causing danger to its rider. How would the pig enjoy what it likes most, wallowing if its legs were longer?

If the dog lost its intelligence, speed and ability to obey its masters commands how would the sheep and in fact other farmyard animals be guided to be where and when the farmer needs them to be. All this should be considered when thinking about evolution, and were haven't started looking at our friends in the wild.

We should start with the giraffe, has a very long neck for eating from tree tops, but was also equipped with long legs so they could reach water for drinking. If we as man continue to destroy his food chain we will have another extinct animal. The elephant on the other hand has the power and weight ratio to simply bring his food to his own level.

Was it by design or chance that the enormous hippopotamus can remain under water and so decrease the opportunity of suffering from the blazing sun and heat? Did those original two plankton of the evolutionists equip the carnivores on our planet with speed, strong jaws and strength? Were certain lizards given the ability to change colour for safety against their predictors?

What I am trying to place before you is that when one questions and uses their ability or talents, evolution reminds us of the famous story of the emperor's new clothes. The moral of that was there were no new clothes. but if you did not see them there was something radically wrong with you.

This was a great confidence trick, but even this was out played by the evolution theory. By the way it took a young innocent child to expose that con, your reasoning and truthful consideration will expose the evolution theory to you. There are forms of evolution that we accept, the egg and the birds, but when considered many of the earth's inhabitants start life as an egg. The Bible points out that every living thing was a product of a creator God.

We also know something has to be added to make that egg fertile to produce off-spring whether it be human, reptile, spider, amphibious or fowl, so the evolution from egg to living creature is complete. I cannot understand that a caterpillar encases itself in a cocoon and later emerges as a moth or beautiful and colourful butterfly, nor do I want that knowledge, to accept the happening is sufficient. There is no need to have answers for every thing that happens, sit back and enjoy the world around us, for we will never know the true mysteries of life in our brief stay here on earth.

We were given enquiring minds and when we look at our advances in medical science, unravelling the mysteries of space, mobility, travel, and discovery, why do we then have to turn to the make believe world of guesswork and exaggeration. Surely it is enough to search and know the world in which we live, rather than go back in time to a world we cannot prove.

I have as yet not touched on the evolutionists time frame, in my life time my experience has shown me a complete framework of a wooden house totally destroyed by termites. As a member of a school committee that had invested in a pine forest for future funding, it faced financial disappointment when it was found that the trees were infested and of no value. We received no income only inherited the cost of removing the trees. If these things can happen in a life time, can we not assume we know very little of the events in the past?

Most of us will never see or hold one million dollars in our hands at any one time, and so a millionaire and a billionaire and all those in between have a life style and bank balance we cannot fathom. Our life expectancy although increasing, is about 80 to 100 years, so how can you explain to me the statements made by evolutionist about the earth's age?

Theories are passed on over ages, but what these evolutionists do not explain is why even before their particular science was born, how and by what method do they use to date plants rocks and animal remains? Do they use methods only discovered in recent times? How do they know these tests are not only effective but give a true and honest answer?

Many professing evolution to be the magical answer to the past, cannot agree on the time frame. We have news services and documentaries quoting from hundreds of million years down a miserable million years. Does such a variance give you confidence to believe? Well many do! Just as many ask me to prove there is a God, let them prove to me their theories, by prove I mean absolute infallible truth. Now to look at the great flood, which, by the way, if I am to believe in histories of other nations recorded by archaeologists, is recorded in all civilisations of that period.

In the years 2012 and the beginning of 2013 monster flooding was recorded in many parts of the world. The eastern coast of Australia from the top of Queensland to central New South Wales was blanketed with above normal rainfall. Queensland suffering extreme flooding twice in three years. The rainfalls triggering these floods lasted only a few weeks, and then not consistent.

But can we imagine rain falling for forty days and nights? The current weather conditions have seen beaches eroded as the sea pushes its boundaries, we have seen mud slides changing the landscape, houses washed away, low laying areas no longer suitable for habitation. I have seen blow-holes eroded in solid rock through the power and consistent battering by river water. There are places where you can see the remains of houses some distance from the sea shore.

All this in under the last 100 years. To name these place, the blow-hole on the Yarra River at Warrandyte, Victoria, the houses all at sea at Crib Island where the new Brisbane airport was built. If the sea can travel and overtake the land in so short a time, why do we have to accept that evolution and the creation of the earth took these millions of years? Could the force of Noah's flood be so great as to carve out the Grand Canyon?

There are many probable answers to the creation and reforming of the earth's surface. We are told to worry about a melt down at the Poles, of how the excess water will flood low laying islands, how earthquakes can still form islands and destroy them also. How volcanoes with their relentless lave flow can destroy whole cities. It has proven most profitable to continue with this myth of pre-historic animals, with tourism, and science, science with government grants and pay cheques, to further their theories.

How can it be justified to spend millions to find water on far away planets when we are not spending this money on ensuring a liveable quantity of water for our brothers and sisters sharing this planet of ours. It is very difficult not to class these people operating the purse strings as being egotistical. They work only for their own well being.

Even today we hear that scientists have cloned an extinct frog, and now feel they have the secret to all life. Their next mission to bring back those gigantic prehistoric beasts, why? When we are loosing present day animals through man's invasion of their food chain. It is simply to gain more funding and perhaps one day to have their names inscribed in their favourite journal?

If there is secret to life it cannot be found in death, we must look for cures for living members of our communities who are suffering from numerous debilitating illnesses. Is it so difficult for learned people to concentrate on established problems instead of creating more by bring back extinct fauna?

Explaining life is complex if you don't believe in a true and living God. At the age of 54 and suffering multiple heart attacks, my wife insisted I attend a local church, new to us. The Pastor commenced by saying there was someone in the congregation with a severe heart problem, I went forward and was prayed over.

The result was amazing. Although 3 years later I underwent a triple by-pass operation, now at 83 and a published author, I have undertaken a series of books, of which this is one.

Christianity today seems to have gone asleep, it has allowed inroads to be established into what we know from Jesus' sojourn on earth. Each Christian will at some time have a personal experience with

Jesus or his Spirit. God gave you a free will to accept or deny the Bible's stories and the promises of God if we obey His laws.

As a child we all accepted what our teachers, and parents tried to teach us, we accepted that we had a choice. Your choice now is do you accept evolution starting from two elements, a big bang, even though you have never been told where these elements came from in the first place.

It is most difficult to believe in a creator being, because our minds are not able to evaluate nothingness, but answer this in all honesty, consider the wonders of your own body! Do you have to time every breath you take? Do you have to manually operate your heart beats or your speech or actions?

Then start here and tell me how if a master designer and engineer did not create you, how could the eye see, the ear hear, the mouth speak, and your body functions keep you nourished, cleansed with an efficient waste disposal unit.

My last words are these, Do not accept any proposal without deep and thoughtful study.

Try **LOOK BEFORE YOU LEAP!**

Some Truths For The Young!

There are many choices available to young people who are so important to the future of the world. That's right, never sell yourselves short, whereas we of the older generation, have nothing to show but selfishness and greed, plunging the world in chaos and warfare, hate, murder, placing even the most humble of people into poverty and perhaps slavery of a new kind.

Yours is a world of what you wish to make it, you may live in perfect friendship and harmony with all those around you, or you can follow those who have gone before and have lost the gift to accept everyone's right to their own personal beliefs.

Beware of what you are taught to believe, without looking at conflicting theories, for how can you make your decisions without knowledge. To say that I, of an older generation do not struggle with modern technology, which children and young adults understand and use with a professionalism, one of my age can only dream about. Some years ago my twelve year old grandson not only designed a cover for a leaflet I was printing, but offered to teach me easier ways to do the computer work at hand.

The question I have to ask the younger generation is simply this, with all that is available to you in the form of entertainment both in the home and outside, why do you turn to dangerous and illegal pastimes?

Why do you need the adrenalin rush through alcohol and/or drugs, which in many cases causes serious injury. One's desire to drive a car can turn to impatience, we then drive illegally, have an accident causing injury or death to yourself or your mates.

Not only do you have to live with this throughout your life, but you may never be able to drive again, so before you make any such decisions, take time out to summarise the worst possible scenario. So you are in a group that decides to have a tattoo, think first, could it effect you future life? A name of a friend of the opposite sex could be embarrassing if the friendship ends and you can't find someone else with the same name.

At 18 you are fit, with a body to be proud of, so you think a sexy girl as a tattoo would impress the boys, so you tell your next girlfriend, who may prove to be you perfect partner for life, it is of her. But at thirty your body is somewhat worse for the wear and tear you have placed upon it, your sexy girl tattoo has also changed and what was once a slim sleek body has gained many kilo's and does not resemble what you were once very proud. What started as a compliment to your loved one has now become an embarrassing insult.

So it's the weekend, your labours at school or work are finished for the week, you have your allowance or wage, after board has been paid to your loving parent or parents you still have money left over. Where to go, in my age it was easy, you were not allowed into a hotel until reaching 21, so you had a movie, a dance, perhaps a concert or to share an evening at a friend's place.

Now you have still the movie theatre, dances usually are at a club or hotel both of which supply liquor, and there are the unscrupulous vendors of drugs lining their pockets with your well earned money. For a short time on a high, you have endangered your whole future life. I smoked and knew I could quit when I wanted, not so, my four artery heart by-pass operation became three, because there was not enough artery left that had not been attacked by smoking.

It is so easy to become addicted to any form of habit, there are of course good and bad habits. Some habits such as saving your money and having an end goal whereon to spend that what you have saved are good.

The opposite to saving is spending, which may give you an adrenalin rush for a short time but when that wears off, you are left thinking was it worth it? Have you worked it out yet that paying cash for what you wish to purchase, will give you bargaining power and a cheaper price.

What would you spend one million dollars plus on, a house, but hang on they are selling for between $300,000 and $500,000, by paying cash, over than a mortgage over thirty years you will save the interest payments which by rule of thumb would treble the initial cost.

How can you save that initial amount, think of the waste in your habits which can become addictions. Cigarettes, alcohol, drugs, tattoos, body piecing and so many of the other things we rage over. Unfortunately there are other objects that can become addictive, music the purchase of CD's and DVD's can soon see the weekly budget diminish. As a Jazz record collector, much of my hard earned cash went on my then addiction.

There was not the television made celebrities, we did of course have movie actors, but although we had our favourites it was most doubtful that we would ever see any of them in the flesh. Air travel had as yet not been the acceptable way of overseas personalities arriving on Australian shores, travel by sea was both lengthy and not up to the comfort expectations of the liners of today.

So as their public appearance was not available because of the distance and time spent on board a ship was enough to keep most of the overseas musicians, actors and celebrities away. If and when they did come the ticket cost for their concerts took most of our earnings. So there was no real addiction to personalities as there is today. There is no doubt that we had our favourites but they were not forced upon as we had no television, and radio was mainly for home and family entertainment and listening to the latest war news.

As young people you may think that the older generation does not truly understand what your problems are and the environment in which you live. On one hand we tell you not to smoke, yet of adult managers of cigarette firms advertise you should smoke, even though they know that they can cause diseases of the lungs, and hearts.

You are told through media advertising that alcohol and driving are hazardous, and yet we see motor sports advertising alcohol, and on the palladium at the end of the race, quantities of champagne are splattered over the place getters and the crowd.

You are informed of the dangers of drug taking and yet the distributors must have access to huge amounts of cash and therefore must be of an age where they can finance importation or local distribution for the drugs they sell. You are subjected to high pressure advertising and in many cases have the finance to buy that which is advertised, but with the increasing crime wave in robberies, bashings, shop lifting and to keep up with those who have the money, you turn to crime.

The pressure of advertising did not exist before the commercialisation of the media. We have tailored all kinds of media to attract buyers of the goods advertised in our publications, newspapers, radio and television. The adult management of these companies who realise that you will buy what they rely on for income and profit for not only the company and shareholders who want a greater return for their investment, than the safety of bank term deposits.

It is the greed of such people that takes from you the finance that will be needed as you grow older, fall in love and wish to commence a family with your soul mate. I regret to remind all young people that it is not what you learn from schools that fits you for the world outside your safe haven called home, it is what you learn from experiences in life.

I am fortunate having lived in an age where cash was the only way to trade. There was of course cheques but because of unscrupulous people these were not always accepted, and the cash from these was limited to what you had in your bank balance.

What you had in your pocket was the extent of what you could purchase. There were lay-bys, and time payment which required a good credit history. Now we have plastic cards both cash or credit, on a cash card you spend your own money, the credit card allows you to spend the banks, which requires interest to be paid.

Examples from life's experiences may be the best way to illustrate this lesson. Your parents conduct a successful business, in this instance let us look at a trade. They have quoted on a house painting job and are successful. The estimate is $10,000 with a progress payment to be made half way through the job. There is a delay in this payment but your parents decide to finish the job and submit the account. The job is finished, but there is a problem, the people have been declared bankrupt or are in receivership.

Your parents have not only forgone the initial money as quoted but now have the materials, labour and all other costs. So instead for loosing $10,000 the total is more like $20,000. So you will not be getting the car as promised and your family is in danger of loosing all they have ever worked for.

In every day life pilfering and shop lifting is becoming a great and costly burden for shop owners who are supplying a service to the community. They may buy an article for $10 and add the cost of wages, rent, taxation, and other costs, and sell it for $20.

But then some one steals one, and we can presume that all up they are making $5 on each item sold. By loosing that one item they have to sell three before they make up what they lost on the stolen article. When I was young I was never told and therefore never realised that every thing that I did had some effect on someone else.

This is even more relevant today, because you have access to lethal weapons that were not available to ordinary people. We weren't pure, for we had the underground gangs that organised the illegal trade, and they had these weapons. But added to knives and guns we now have the car, motor cycle, and extreme sports all that can be very lethal. Youth sex was not so prevalent as it is today.

We have sex education in schools, we did not have this in years gone by. If this is a good thing or not, in itself, time only will tell. Add to this television shows which shows school girls being sexually active with adults and a school boy likewise with his female teacher.

We can listen and see some of our television personalities and sporting celebrities acting in a manner which would bring lesser known people into disrepute. If I can raise a question for all young people to think about and answer within their understanding, it would be this.

Which is the most dangerous, driving a motor vehicle under trained, under the influence of alcohol or drugs, excessive speed or even sending messages or telephoning while driving, or having unsafe sex?

In school sex education are our youth taught responsibility, or because of the promiscuous attitude of some teenagers do boys now believe that all females are fair game for their sexual advances? Whereas once every public toilet had an enamel plaque on the wall, warning of possible sexual disease infection, one was left with the wonder of just what was it all about.

Perhaps two very important issues are neglected from your lessons on sex. The first is respect, the second is control over your emotions. I for one, could never deny that I was sexually attracted to my wife, in our years of courting. Because I respected her desire to control what happened to her body, I had to also learn control.

The sex relations boarders have been broadened, we now have a rising homosexual group who wish to be accepted by the broader community. We did know that homosexuality existed and did so back in Biblical times. I had personal friend who was homosexual, but it did not become a part of every day discussions. I was straight and he was homosexual but it never interfered with our friendship or social behaviour.

As we live in one society, no one should or even must have dominance over any other, we were created equal, but life treats us in different ways. If you come from a prominent family you will find it easier to cope with trials as the present themselves. Such families do not have only financial resources to help, but also have contacts in prominent places for advice.

Life today is far more complex than it was once, people kept within themselves their own personal feelings on many matters. You would not know once how your neighbour voted or if they supported a political party. Now when leaving a polling booth you may be asked who you voted for. Again I cannot say if this the way of the future, but be assured one's openness will be controlled and your inner most secrets laid bare.

The greatest lesson in life to be learnt, is that in one second our lives change or can be changed, one mistake, one bad decision can alter your life from joyousness to tragedy. From life to death, from fit and well, to being so handicapped your reliance on others for every natural act is your future existence.

Your impatience to drive a motor vehicle before adequate training and then experience, can cause accidents and injuries even death to you, your friends and even innocent by-standers. Your earnest desire to have one more alcoholic drink, one more dose of drug taking may be your last.

If only those young friends who have departed this life had thought of the consequences their full life expectancy could have achieved, but it was cut short. For every action no matter how small, at the moment of decision will have a consequence.

Run your race with endeavour but with caution. You may make mistakes, but if you learn from them and file them under experience your future pathway will be worth the effort.

DO NOT READ THIS IF YOU THINK THESE THINGS WILL NOT EFFECT YOUR FUTURE LIFE!

The Black Angel!

The Book of Revelation, chapter 12 and verse 7 to 9, *"And there was war in heaven, Michael and his angels fought against the dragon, and the dragon and his angels fought back. But he was not strong enough, and they lost their place in heaven. The great dragon was hurled down - that ancient serpent called the devil, or Satan, who leads the whole world astray. He was hurled to the earth, and his angels with him."*

This portion of scripture leaves no opening for questioning or doubts, there is a great spiritual battle going on between good and evil. Every one who has ever lived or is yet to be born will have a part in it, no one past, present or future will be exempt. There are many good things happening but the evil around us is overpowering us because we as Christians do not take up the sword of the Spirit, we remember turn the other cheek rather than Paul's Armour of God prayer.

Ephesians chapter 6 and verses 10 to 20, with particular emphasis on verse 17, *"Take the helmet of salvation and the sword of the spirit, which is the word of God."* The sword is a weapon of attack, and never a war has been won without aggression or by turning our other cheek. We are left in no doubt who the dragon is, he is called by every name he was known by, the devil, Satan, and serpent. We as earth dwellers now know that he is our fellow earth dweller, the black angel and his army of deposed and defeated angels.

Where we fail, is that we do not remind them when we are tempted, that they have been defeated by the same Jesus who we believe in and follow. Lets define some points, there is and always has been good and bad, turn the cheek or revenge, constructive and destructive.

As a Christian I believe that God leads all that is good, and because of his complete destructive actions Satan or the evil one, is as said, evil or bad. God gave Adam and Eve a garden of perfection, and it has been recorded that Satan as the serpent destroyed the faith that God had in His creation in human form, and that great gift was removed forever.

If you are not of God then you are of the evil one, the choice is yours, but be very aware what evil, hatred and even horror is perpetrated by Satan and his dark angels. The marshal arts, may teach how to defend oneself, but when we cage two men in a ring, encourage them to beat, harm and hate enough to do physical damage, it then transforms men into servants of Satan.

Law makers pass laws protecting roosters from cock fighting, dogs from tearing each other to pieces, and yet allow men and in some cases women and children to build up such an ambition to be the number one in so called sports which cause damage to other humans.

Those irresponsible people who take control of motor vehicles when under the influence of drugs, alcohol, of known illness and cause innocent people to suffer injuries and even death, are worthy servants of the black angel, and will receive their just rewards.

Those weekend reports of fights, stabbings, of people who just want to relax on a quiet night out, please the black angel no end, for, he has a victory by destroying lives which in other circumstances could be examples of what goodness and love would achieve. Let us go from the violence of the present day world, violence that is fast approaching that of ancient Rome, with its cauldron of death, the battle to the death of gladiators, whose lives depended on the position of the spectators thumb.

Battles to the death between men, and men against wild animals, chariot-races that brought death and destruction to man and horses, these all for the so-called pleasure of the masses. The morbid fascination for seeing our fellow man killed or seriously injured has not abated, boxing, wrestling, contact sports, bull riding, all of which cause discomfort to both man and beast have a growing following. Parents are introducing their offspring to become spectators and therefore future devotees of these black angel dominated destructive events.

There are other areas where Satan has great success, the finance and banking industry. No matter how we view it, is a necessity. There is a governing banking force which tries to regulate interest rates on present day monetary trends, it is then left to individual banking organisations to set a figure for interest rates on credit cards and mortgages. The main excuse in their adjusting the rates is to keep their investors income at a reasonable level, and forget about all those who are effected by mortgage interest rate rises.

The Satanic influences come in when millions are paid out in wages and bonuses to top executives who will not spend it in a life time and it will not be usable in their future after death. Two families living as neighbours, one family has shareholding in a bank that raises its mortgage rates and they cheer, the other have their loan through the same bank and become destitute, who then are the followers of the black angel?

One man has worked hard and amassed a fortune, builds a palatial home, swimming pool and every imaginable convenience, a couple of top of the range cars, boat, bank balance and investments, he no doubt has worked hard and prospered. Another has worked hard had not had the opportunities to establish his fortune. Marriage, children, health, lack of job security has made him a battler. Although not lamenting his lot in life, he does wish and covert some of those assets of his neighbour. Satan places jealousy in his heart; he breaks the commandments, by coveting an other's lifestyle. Who then is the greatest servant of the devil, the one that has and keeps all he has above what he needs, or the man who has jealousy in his heart? This is the double-edged sword of the black angel. The question then rises, how much is too much? When does need become greed?

Why should one man have millions and another not enough for a cup of tea or coffee? Why should there be excess of money spent on drugs, alcohol, cigarettes, entertainment, perks to public servants, bonuses to those who really do not need them and who receive ample without them?

Why do many have no place to sleep, no place to shelter or food to eat, no doctor or hospital treatment available when ill or old? Why is 440 million USD spent on bombing the moon in search of water, and 340 USD million spent on placing a new telescope in orbit? Millions are spent on the whims and wishes of the scientific community.

Why is it that thousands go without pure water, medication, health services in third world countries, when only a portion of the money wasted on scientific projects which do nothing or prove nothing, and advance the living conditions of man, this should be used for their well being.

Why should the leaders of some countries have comfortable aircraft with sleeping facilities, when many of their people have no where to sleep? The answer of course, is in the lead up scripture to this chapter, "He, the black angel (Satan) was hurled to the earth, and his angels with him.

We live in Satan's kingdom but that does not mean we are his or that we have to follow his regime, that is why God gave us a free will. We can and must choose between good of God and the black angel's evil, what ever we deny others, when we look the other way when others are in trouble, when we look the other way when our friends need support these are things that give pleasure to the black angel and his followers.

Whenever we remain silent about our love for our Saviour, we without doubt are serving the prince of darkness. The heart of the black angel is one that rejoices in the destruction of all that is Holy and Good. In my life lately, even after so many years after giving my life to Jesus, and so many instances when I have seen and been a part of God's gracious gifts called miracles, why am I cast into depression through lack of faith?

But is it a lack of faith or the doubt I have in answering calls for action I receive during the night? I firmly believe that I have been called to commence a local Christian Newspaper, but because of lack of support and the division between the Spiritual Leaders of the different congregations it has never come to fruition although finance was available to print an initial copy.

I was lead to believe that a established property was available for sale and would have made a great youth camp. Most people I talked to agreed with me, but as it was some 300 kilometres away, and the family decided to sell its usable assets and decided to sell or rent the property.

It then became uneconomical to pursue the matter further. Interest came from people in my area and very little from the area where the property existed. Did I misunderstand what I believe was God's calling, or is Satan's hold on people of today so great that his will can be done with little prayer or dissent from those professing to be in the Christian army.

If Satan can make believers doubt what is God's will, just how far away is the prophesy in the Book of Revelation, chapter 20: 7-10. ***"When the thousand year are over, Satan will be released from his prison and will go out to deceive the nations in the four corners of the earth - Gog and Magog - to gather them for battle. in number they are like the sand on the seashore. They marched across the breadth of the earth and surrounded the camp of God's people, the city He loves, but fire came down from heaven and devoured them.***

And the devil, who deceives them, was thrown into the lake of burning sulphur, where the beast and the false prophet had been thrown. They will be tormented day and night for ever and ever."

This is proof of the black angel's knowledge of how our minds work, especially the minds consecrated to God, for once before he succumbed to the search for power and the overthrow of the Almighty God, when he was also a servant to God. What do you think when you read of the inhuman behaviour that happens on our streets over the weekend?

We blame alcohol, drugs, thuggery, the big man syndrome, which unfortunately has reached into the actions of our women, and look past the one one who has control of these poor souls. These acts are performed by young people, but the puppeteer is the wily old serpent of Adam and Eve's first sin.

In case the names by which he has been known have become too familiar, lets call him by the name that in this day and age aptly describes him, "the black angel." We live in an age where we have Super Heroes to guard us from evil, but unfortunately these are in our imagination and their fight against evil is not real.

Revelation 13:18, *"This calls for wisdom. If anyone has insight, let him calculate the number of the beast, for it is man's number. His number is 666."* We have seen in movie made about the beast, where his human form had the number 666 on his head but covered by hair, which places all evil on one body. Not so, consider this, if as some ancient civilisations and even in the twentieth century, the number seven had a special meaning. Some believe seven was perfection, others particularly gamblers that it was lucky, and who knows what Hitler believed, after all he used four to make up his national emblem.

If we then take the special significance seven has, and presume that it stands for perfection, and we find that the number of the beast, Satan, the black angel is **666**, we can surmise that being just under 700, would be a little less than perfect. We now can correctly assume that the black angel was less than perfect, but we can also understand how very simply we can fall from perfection in the Holy Spirit to the evil that is Satan, the fall is not that far. We may attend our preferred worship, Bible study, prayer groups, volunteer for activities or leading in the Church operation, but all can be in vain if we desire to gain power in the community when all power belongs to God.

We should remember that this was the thinking of Satan before his rebellion against God, power could be his, things could be different if only he was the leader. As this brought the great spiritual war into being, so will the selfish desires of evil ones when they presume that their way is more better than the Christian way, and bring the world into chaos and disrepute.

Tie-in the ends of knowledge together, we know that Satan was perhaps second in command in heaven, we know he was the leader of music, and are told of times when God was meeting with his angels, Satan attended, we do not know if he was invited or not. Read for yourselves from the Book of Job chapter 1 : 6 to 12.

"One day the angels came to present themselves before the Lord, and Satan also came with them. The Lord said to Satan,'Where have you come from?' Satan answered the Lord, 'From roaming through the earth and going to and fro in it.' Then the Lord said to Satan, 'Have you considered my servant Job? There is no one on earth like him, he is blameless and upright, a man who fears God and shuns evil.'

'Does Job fear God for nothing?' Satan replied. Have you not put a hedge around him and his household and every thing he has? You have blessed the work of his hands, so that his flocks and herds are spread throughout the land. But stretch out your hand and strike everything he has, and he will surely curse you to your face.' The Lord said to Satan,' Very well, then, everything he has is in your hands, but on the man himself do not lay a finger.' Then Satan went out from the presence of the Lord.

The Book of Job as printed establishes many truths that can be overlooked as we witness the trials of this blameless and upright man who was dedicated to his God. Firstly it shows what great faith God has in his human creation. It also shows the evil intent that Satan has and how he is prepared to use it to destroy the fellowship between God and man.

It also proves that God does not punish man while earthly life exists, this is left to the Black Angel. It contains the audacity of Satan to stand up to and argue against God. We can now find that Satan was not excluded from meetings of the angels, and that his eviction from heaven to earth did take place, for as he states in verse 7, **"From roaming through the earth and going to and fro in it."** For all those who do not believe in Satan, be assured he and his disciples are living and active in the everyday world of today.

It is so easy to lay all our problems upon God, when we do not accept that there is a Black Angel who has mustered forces from ordinary people who consciously or unconsciously serve him without question.

I must confess that I, more than once, have believed I knew better than my Master, and perhaps was critical of His handling of the problems of the world, of course these are implants of the black angel, but when reason returns, I admit that the world's problems are caused by my fellow world dwellers.

The mess is ours and we must confess and work diligently to right all the wrongs perpetrated though our disobedience to God. Truth must again be the base of our religion, we have to preach Christ and Him Crucified, there is no other defence from the evil that surrounds all humanity, perpetrated by the black angel through those who aspirations lie in the accumulation of wealth, power and self above all else.

We as Christians believe that the God we worship is in every good thing that happens, and is therefore every where at all times through the Holy Spirit of Christ, but when will we recognise the power of the black angel, that he is able to tempt me at the same time as destroying the souls of countless thousands throughout the world.

We must realise that to defeat a power such as his, we must rely upon the power of One who has already over come his tempting and through the resurrection has defeated the black angels most intricate plan, the death of Jesus the true Son of God.

This requires a fully consecrated and united army ready and equipped to follow our leader Jesus Christ in every way and every where He wishes to lead us. There can be no lasting victory over the black angel until all our earthly Christian resources are mobilised as one force, and all our truth, dedication, passion and love is at the disposal of the only One who is able to lead us against a very formidable foe.

As we as followers of Christ know and accept that God has shown and proven that to Him all things are possible, we must never try to face the black angel with out the power of Christ's Spirit within us, without the certainty of this Spirit, not a replica of the cross or even Holy Water will deter Satan for his complete destruction of an unprepared soul.

The Large Millstone

For two reasons this chapter has been included, the first because it contains a warning from God's Son whilst he was on earth, and the second, because of mechanical means, very few of us would know what a millstone was or is.

But first some Scripture. Saint Matthews's Gospel, chapter 18 and verses 1 through to 8: *At that time the disciples came to Jesus and asked, "Who is the greatest in the kingdom of heaven?" He called a little child and had him stand among them. And he said, "I tell you the truth, unless you change and become as little children, you will never enter the kingdom of heaven. Therefore, who ever humbles himself like this child is the greatest in the kingdom of heaven. And who ever welcomes a little child like this in my name welcomes me. But if anyone causes one of these little ones who believe in me to sin, it would be better for him to have a large millstone hung around his neck and to be drowned in the depths of the sea. Woe unto the world because of the things that cause people to sin! Such things must come, but woe to the man through whom they come!"*

If only every one read this portion of scripture, child abuse, forced child labour, murder, torment would not exist and child protection agencies not needed. It may be now time to clarify some points in the scripture reading. A millstone was a very heavy stone wheel used for grinding grain. In some cases it was moved by donkeys tethered by harness in a circular fashion. If we turn our Bibles back to the book of Judges, we find that after being subdued by the Philistines, Sampson was taken into captivity. Judges chapter 16 and verse 21, **Then the Philistines seized him, gouged out his eyes and took him down to Gaza. Binding him with bronze shackles, they set him to grinding in the prison.**

From this we can see that there would be no escape from having a weight such as this around your neck, Jesus stipulated that it was to be a large millstone, but that also the perpetrator was to be drowned in the depths of the sea.

Revelation tells in chapter 20 and verses 12 and 13, **And I saw the dead, great and small, standing before the throne and books were opened. Another book was opened, which is the book of life. The dead were judged according to what they had done as recorded in the books. The sea gave up the dead that were in it, and death and Hades gave up the dead that were in them, and each person was judged according to what he had done.**

The main point of interest in this reading is that even after being drowned in the depth of the sea they will still face judgement, and they will make it just before those already residing in Hades. This chapter will make you aware of just who have placed obstacles in the paths of children, and at some stage, if honest, we have deprived children of their standing in the eyes of Jesus and his Father's heaven.

This brings us to a point of interest, as Adam and Eve were perfect before eating the fruit and gaining the knowledge of good and evil, in the reading from Matthew, Jesus endorsed the certainty that until little ones who were perfect before gaining knowledge and believed in him were of such they would be welcome in the kingdom of heaven.

In the world today there are many temptations that surround our youth, most if not all placed there by some of the older generation who care not for a child's life but only for financial gain, and so in destroying young lives, continue the work of Satan and his evil disciples.

It matters not at what age evil people seek to destroy young lives by promising the material things of this world, for this is all that Satan has and controls and so can promise. Let us now look of those thousands upon thousands who deserve and will be rewarded with that millstone.

From the very beginning of our lives we are reliant on others to teach and train us to live worthy lives, to appreciate friendships, and to have love and compassion for all around us. Unfortunately those entrusted with our spiritual and physical well being have neither the inclination, the desire or the knowledge of how that education should be administered.

So we find ourselves trusting and believing in people, although very close to us to the Lord God and His Son Jesus Christ. Although in each home the will be a Bible it is never opened. Possibly the only time we shall enter a church building is at our naming, which is a service where many promises are made to God on our behalf and very few are kept by the family or even the congregation. Consider the number of millstones already needed and this happens before we, as a child can comprehend good and evil.

Parents and Godparents, all members of the congregation, to officiating Clergy are all making promises, through prayers to God, which we either have no intention of keeping or cannot because of lack of knowledge of what exactly God requires of us.

Does it make a difference if we are nurtured in a Christian household or not? My father was born into a Methodist family, they worshipped in a family church. My dad and his brothers left their mark in that church, probably not spiritually as their father desired, but with their initials carved in the back of the pews. When my father became an adult and could choose his own way, he chose freedom from the strict Methodist upbringing.

The consequences of this was that I was not brought up in a Christian home and learned of God through religious education at school and a very limited Sunday School experience. Like wise my wife was not brought up in a practising Christian home, in both cases there was a caring and loving relationship between child and parents. The failure to include Christianity into the education of children, surely earned parents a millstone. Fortunately I was found, became a Christian, later my wife also gave her life to Christ and was baptised.

I am not at all jealous of those who were included in a family that worshipped god, for we have had experiences which have proven, without argument, the great love and interest of a God that truly cares. Not all has been plain sailing, but no matter what the seriousness of the trials, we have always finished blessed.

The next experience for young lives includes the actions of friends, school acquaintances, even in some cases, family. There are many depths of persecution, from verbal to political, mental and physical, there seems to create a great exuberance in some who would destroy one's faith in a God, that Christians know from experience, does exist.

It is difficult to know just what these persecutors gain or achieve or if they have the real feeling of serving their master Satan. If God's kingdom looses any one of these who believe in Christ Jesus, by the actions of any of these persecutors, it were better that a millstone be hanged about their necks and they were drowned in the depths of the sea.

Then it is our social life, perhaps through our sporting endeavours, our work place, even in our home or social life, unless we are strong in the Spirit of Christ, then we stand in jeopardy of loosing a Saviour, true friend who loves and cares for us. Those who allow Satan to use for his evil and destructive purposes, will receive a millstone as a permanent necklace, but beware, every step of our Christian life is under attack by the old serpent and his army, the devil and disciples.

Now it is the musicians, the composers, the owners of recording companies, and don't forget the shareholders who make money by not censoring the material they offer. Their actions are responsible for destroying the morals of our very important young. We have commentators who will advertise such material and artists that perform in a questionable way, these too are candidates for rock jewellery.

In the movie and television industries the same applies, all those who seem to believe that without insidious sexual escapades, gruesome horror and murders, episodes will not be acceptable to those whose money provides them with a more than adequate financial return. But, be warned, writers, programmers, producers, advertisers and actors, for your tainting of the young minds, woe awaits you, perhaps not in this life but there is an after life, change now and stop corroding the morals of the multitudes.

The fashion industry is also not immune or exempt, for its participation in designing clothing for young girls, which in all cases is not appropriate, and places extremely young girls in jeopardy from sick minds. We now find that what fashion decrees, not only makes fortunes for designers, models, manufacturers and retail outlets in that field, but also does its best to remove modesty from their word bank.

It has now spread faster than a childhood epidermic, upon a time, when money was scarce and clothing material was expensive, skirts and shorts covered waistlines and modesty made sure the posterior was well and truly covered. Shirts and blouses had enough material to cover the top of the lower garment.

Some how the modesty and morals of pregnant women has escaped all decency, as women many months into their pregnancy have a large gap between the bottom of the upper garment and the top of the lower garment. They seem to forget, that although my wife's five pregnancies, (one set of twins), were a joy for me to behold, to see women parading around shopping centre without shame or humility, fills many with shame and embarrassment.

There are of course other options provided the question of morals does not arise, there are strip clubs, photo shoots, pornographic movies, where cast off model can be used as nothing better than utensils for making money. These people who are drawn into these distasteful and disgusting acts, are not the only ones damaged.

There are those who are drawn to the web, magazines and other outlets that rely on sexual filth to gain earthly riches. There is a big difference between love and lust. All those so involved should heed the warning and take the advice offered by Jesus of not earning a millstone.

A warning from Leviticus 19 – 28, **"Do not cut your bodies for the dead or put tattoo marks on yourselves. I am the Lord."** We should now look at the growing industry of tattoo and body piecing, God did create a perfect human body and to think that we can improve what He has made is perhaps the greatest insult we can bestow on a gracious and loving God. To desecrate the smoothness of skin by sometimes decorative, sometimes obscene and sometimes blasphemous illustrations and always contrary to God's wishes.

These businesses have been born and continue to expand by people who are unaware of the rules that we will be judged by eventually. They are driven by greed for material assets, and these last only as long as we live on earth, and only God knows how long that will be.

Could this be the introduction to a new and perhaps lucrative business, selling millstones. There is in this world so much selfishness that we forget or ignore the damage that is done by the youth of today. Unless you seek out the type and number of stumbling blocks we place in the pathways of Christian youth, Satan's plans will prosper and those involved will be looking to wear that millstone necklace.

Sitting in a large shopping complex waiting for my wife, I was astounded by three things I witnessed. How many people of both sexes proudly displaying their personal art work. Others with pieces of metal or jewellery hanging out of various section of what normally was a handsome or beautiful face. Tongues, made for praising God, Eyebrows made to protect the eyes that daily witness the beauty of God's creation, noses made to smell the blossoms of flowers in their season.

All have been subjected to the decrees of fashion of today, all those prospering from this trade should realise they are participating in the desecration of God's perfect design and hand craft made in His own image. Are you being rewarded for participating in these fads? If so strengthen your neck.

Why do we seek to change our bodies? Why do we waste money on so many things that do not comply with the wishes of God? You may not realise or like the reason, but it is simply because we have been sucked in by the greatest confidence trick of all time. We have believed the evil one, the Devil, who cannot tell the truth nor wants you to have the satisfaction and be content with the gifts you have received.

Answer this! Is it worth following false promises to achieve things of this world? How much in earthly money are you willing to expend to follow leaders who know or care nothing about the after life, which extends till and throughout eternity.

The third thing noticed was the increasing number of mothers with children, yet have no witness of marriage by the significant wedding ring. Young expectant mothers who look like school girls, again without seeking God's blessing of Holy Matrimony. All these things are great if these is no God and no life after death.

If these is a God and His Son did live and die for our sins on the cross, then repentance becomes a necessity and a life lived for God's glory and the extension of His earthly kingdom becomes the passport to heaven and eternal life.

Politicians have to accept the blame for many temptations to our youth of today, in Australia a former government moved that a baby bonus be paid as an incentive for women to have babies. There was no provision for marriage or a established partnership be a part of the format. The first and major sin in this is simply that it takes the love desire for a child and changes it to lust for money.

There are now many babies being born who will live their lives without male and female parental love and will grow up neglected and undisciplined the same as their illegitimate parents. Why then was there no fore thought in stipulating this bonus be for married or even de-facto relationships?

The blame and millstone for this rests not only on the author of the programme, but on all those who voted for the scheme and who have not since bothered to change the law to comply with the expected moral standards. Christians are responsible for those they elect into power, These questions should be answered to our satisfaction before we bestow power on any candidate.

It is important that no matter how a political party's agenda suits ours, we must vote for the one who has Christian and moral standards that are parallel to our own. They must believe in the one living God, His Son as Saviour of the world, and uphold, or at least try to uphold the principles of the examples Jesus left us.

They should live out the sanctity of marriage, recognise all the sacraments, and be prepared to stand up for the underprivileged.

They must never be selfish by accepting any perks not available to the poorest of their constituents, then and only then will we be able to trust those thrust into power. I sincerely pray that this chapter will awaken all, be you Christian, Muslim, Agnostic or follow any other religions of the world.

The God I serve has proved many times that He is aware of us and has enormous compassion for our well being. I believe without reservation that He replaced to original sin offering found in Leviticus 6 – 24 onwards, in which that sacrifice was deemed most holy, with the most holy sacrifice of Jesus Christ His only Son, sinless, pure, the lamb without blemish. Jesus was the only worthy one to atone for all the sin in the world.

Unless all the people on earth repent, and as Nineveh did in the book of Jonah, and seek redemption as the whole Christian fellowship, then I fear that the plagues of Revelation will soon be upon us. Unfortunately and using the reading from Matthew, I find heaven may never be overcrowded with the present day dwellers of the earth, the violence against one and another, the destruction of our youth by drugs, alcohol, and lack of instruction on morals and other human beings rights.

The desecration of the beautiful human body, by tattoos, jewellery, the bearing of children not for the purpose proposed by God, but for financial gain. We have all sinned and fallen short of the glory of God, so this leaves the acceptance of the gift of salvation as our decision. Will you now accept the salvation purchased for you on the cross of Calvary, or is that millstone your choice?

PLEASE DO NOT BECOME A WEARER OF THAT LARGE MILLSTONE NECKLACE, FOR IT BECOME MOST UNCOMFORTABLE!

www.ingramcontent.com/pod-product-compliance
Lightning Source LLC
LaVergne TN
LVHW041543060526
838200LV00037B/1121